Y0-AGK-248

SCIENCE PUZZLERS

Solving Science Mysteries

Science Action Labs

Written by Edward Shevick

Illustrated by Marguerite Jones

Teaching & Learning Company

1204 Buchanan St., P.O. Box 10
Carthage, IL 62321-0010

This book belongs to

_____

The activity portrayed on the front cover is described on page 45.

Cover design by Kelly Bollin

Copyright © 1998, Teaching & Learning Company

ISBN No. 1-57310-138-9

Printing No. 987654321

Teaching & Learning Company
1204 Buchanan St., P.O. Box 10
Carthage, IL 62321-0010

The purchase of this book entitles teachers to make copies for use in their individual classrooms only. This book, or any part of it, may not be reproduced in any form for any other purposes without prior written permission from the Teaching & Learning Company. It is strictly prohibited to reproduce any part of this book for an entire school or school district, or for commercial resale.

All rights reserved. Printed in the United States of America.

TLC10138 Copyright © Teaching & Learning Company, Carthage, IL 62321-0010

Table of Contents
Science Action Labs

Dear Teacher or Parent,

The spirit of Sir Isaac Newton will be with you and your students in this book. Newton loved science, math and experimenting. He explained the laws of gravity. He demonstrated the nature of light. He discovered how planets stay in orbit around our sun.

Science Puzzlers can help your students in many ways. Choose some puzzlers to spice up your class demonstrations. Some puzzlers can be converted to hands-on lab activities for the entire class. Some can be developed into student projects or reports. Every class has a few students with a special zest for science. Encourage them to pursue some puzzlers on their own.

Enjoy these Science Puzzlers as much as Newton would have. They are designed to make your students **think**. Thinking and solving problems are what science is all about. Each puzzle is set up as a problem to encourage thought. Students are then asked to come up with their best and most reasonable guess as to what will happen in the puzzler. Scientists call this type of guess a **hypothesis**. Then students are told how to assemble the materials necessary to actually try each puzzler. Scientists call this **experimenting**.

Don't expect the experiments to always prove the hypothesis right. These science puzzlers have been picked to challenge students' thinking abilities.

All the puzzlers in this book are based upon science principles. Many are explained by Newton's laws. That is why Sir Isaac Newton has been used as a guide through the pages of this book. Newton will help your students think about, build and experiment with these puzzlers. Newton will be with them in every puzzler to advise, encourage and praise their efforts.

The answers to the puzzlers are on pages 61-64. You will also find some science facts that will help your students understand what happened.

Here are some suggestions to help your students succeed in solving the puzzlers:

1. Observe carefully.
2. Follow directions.
3. Measure carefully.
4. Hypothesize intelligently.
5. Experiment safely.
6. Keep experimenting until they succeed.

Sincerely,

Ed

Edward Shevick

TLC10138 Copyright © Teaching & Learning Company, Carthage, IL 62321-0010

Rolling into Space

Newton's Puzzler Description

Newton has placed two full soda cans on a table. Each can has an arrow marked on it which is pointing down. A yardstick is placed over both cans. The zero end of the yardstick is lined up exactly with the end of the table.

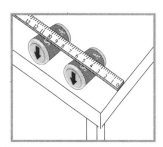

What's the Problem?

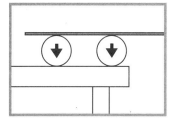

The yardstick will be rolled over the cans until the cans make a **full turn** of 360°. How many inches (centimeters) will the yardstick extend outward from the table after the cans turn completely around?

What Do You Think Will Happen?

As usual, Newton wants you to solve the puzzle mentally before actually trying it. Here are some helpful hints.

1. You can find the can's circumference by measuring its diameter and using the formula πD (π x Diameter). Example: A can with a 2" (5 cm) diameter works out to be 3.14 (π) x 2 = 6.28 inches (15.7 cm).

2. You can use a piece of string to measure the can's circumference directly.

3. Write your estimate for the yardstick's extension beyond the table. _____ inches (cm)

TLC10138 Copyright © Teaching & Learning Company, Carthage, IL 62321-0010

Name _____

How to Build Newton's Puzzler

1. Obtain two soda cans and a yardstick.

2. Mark an arrow on the bottom of each can.

3. Place the yardstick over the cans. The zero end of the yardstick should be lined up **exactly** with the table end.

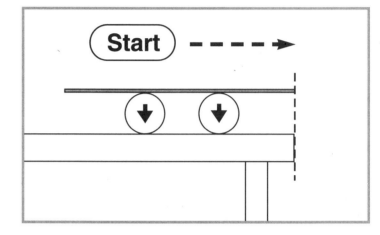

4. Adjust the cans with the arrows pointing down. The cans shouldn't be too close to the end of the table. Readjust the yardstick so it is lined up **exactly** with the table.

5. Push down slightly on the yardstick and roll it toward the table end.

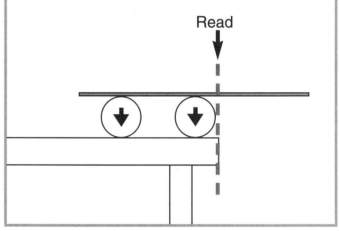

6. Stop rolling when the cans have made **one complete revolution**.

7. Read, in inches (centimeters), the distance the yardstick extends out. _____ inches (cm)

Newton has fooled a lot of people with this puzzler. Before you look in the answer key to find out why your prediction was so far off, try to outsmart the puzzler. You now know how far the board really sticks out. Compare that to your estimate in "What Do You Think Will Happen?" Doesn't that distance give you a clue as to what must have happened?

TLC10138 Copyright © Teaching & Learning Company, Carthage, IL 62321-0010

Balloon Puzzlers

Newton Lost His Balloon

Newton had many balloons at his last birthday party. His favorite was a blue balloon with his name on it. It got free and drifted skyward.

Will Newton's balloon get bigger, smaller or remain the same size as it

rises? _____

_____

Happy Birthday, Newton!

Balloon in a Bottle

Newton thought that it would look festive to have his birthday balloons blown up inside bottles. The sketch to the right shows what Newton did.

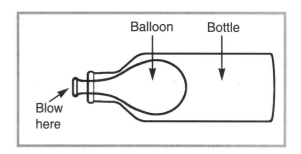

Balloon   Bottle

Blow here

Will Newton be able to blow up a balloon in a bottle? _____

Try the experiment yourself.

What are your results? _____

_____

_____

Newton learned how to blow up a balloon in a bottle. He used a common straw to help him.

How do you think Newton blew up his balloon using a straw? _____

_____

_____

Try it yourself. If you fail, look in the answer key for help.

Name _____

Balloon Blowing Competition

At Newton's birthday party there were plenty of balloons. Newton gave his friends a scientific challenge. He asked his guests to find a way to blow up a balloon *without* using the air in their breath.

You are going to accept Newton's challenge.

1. Work in teams to find unique and different ways of blowing up a balloon.

2. Check your plans with an adult before actually trying your experiment.

3. Use the balloon blowing competition outline below.

   a. Describe your plan in words. _____

   _____

   _____

   b. Make a clear sketch of how your experiment will look.

   c. Get signed approval from an adult. _____ approved

   d. Describe the results of your balloon experiment. _____

   _____

   _____

   _____

Remember that in science, failure is an acceptable result.

Newton Hint: Think of some things that fizz or make bubbles in bread.

TLC10138 Copyright © Teaching & Learning Company, Carthage, IL 62321-0010

Magnetic Mystery

Newton's Puzzler Description

You have a bar magnet and an iron bar. Both are the exact size, shape, weight and color. There are no visible differences between the bar magnet and the non-magnetized iron bar.

What's the Problem?

How can you tell which is the magnet and which is the iron bar? **You cannot use anything but the magnet and the iron bar to determine which is which.** You **cannot** use paper clips, strings to suspend the bars, tools or scientific instruments.

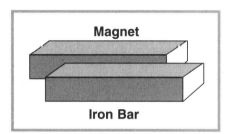

Magnet

Iron Bar

What Do You Think Will Happen?

What are some of your ideas to solve this Newton puzzle? List them.

_____

_____

How to Solve Newton's Puzzler

It is almost impossible to find a bar magnet and an iron bar that are exactly alike. So you are going to have to solve this puzzler without any equipment except your sharp, scientific mind.

Newton suggests you look up the characteristics of magnets in an encyclopedia or textbook for some clues. Scientists often do a lot of reading and research before they tackle a problem.

Name _____

Can Your Eyes Be Fooled?

 ## Newton's Puzzler Description

Newton likes to fool people with optical illusions. His favorite illusion is on the right. Your eyes will shift from seeing one object to another.

Nature has its own optical illusion. Newton reminds you that both the sun and the moon appear larger than normal when they are low on the horizon rather than above you in the sky.

You will be asked to outsmart some famous optical illusions by using your superb powers of observation.

 ## Optical Decisions

Observe the circles below. Which numbered circle is **exactly** the same size as the circle in the shaded area?

Your guess _____

After measuring _____

Observe the lines marked A, B, C, D, E. Which line will go through the space and meet line X?

Your guess _____

After measuring _____

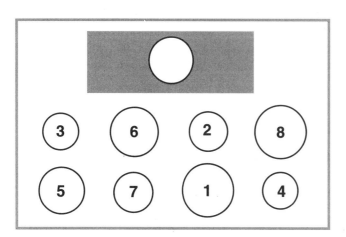

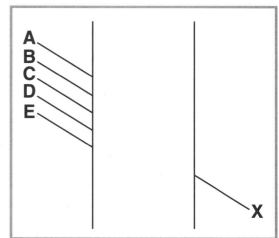

TLC10138 Copyright © Teaching & Learning Company, Carthage, IL 62321-0010

Name _____

Can Lines Fool You?

Nothing really happens in this puzzler. It's just you trying to outsmart some optical illusions. Which two of the six illusions have unequal lines? _____

Observe the six illusions carefully. No rulers, please! Which four of the six have lines A and B that are equal? Give your answers below.

1. _____   2. _____   3. _____

4. _____   5. _____   6. _____

Now measure them with a ruler. Give the results below.

1. _____   2. _____   3. _____

4. _____   5. _____   6. _____

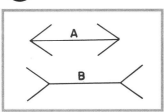
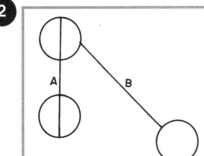
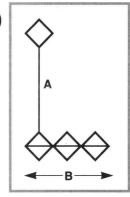
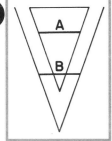
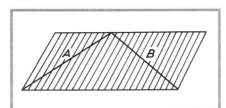
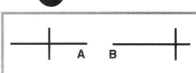

Design some of your own optical illusions. Can you hide some lines in them that could fool your friends?

Name _____

Defying Gravity

Newton's Puzzler Description

This puzzler seems to defy the laws of gravity. A double cone is allowed to roll on a special ramp. The ramp is wider at one end. The ramp is also slightly higher at the wide end. Study the puzzler at the right.

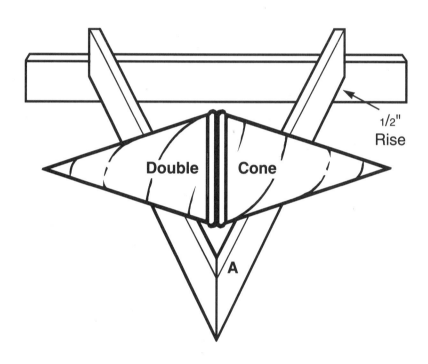

Double | **Cone**

1/2"
Rise

A

What's the Problem?

What will the double cone do when placed at the lower end of the ramp labeled A?

What Do You Think Will Happen?

Will the cone stay at the lower end? Will it roll uphill against gravity? Will it stop at the center?

TLC10138 Copyright © Teaching & Learning Company, Carthage, IL 62321-0010

Name _____

How to Build Newton's Puzzler

1. Obtain two large similar funnels.

2. Tape them together at the wide ends.

3. Obtain two yardsticks and place them on two books as shown below. The book at the wide end should be about 1/2" (1.25 cm) thicker so that the ramp is uphill.

4. Adjust the width between the yardsticks to accommodate the funnel size.

5. Place the double cone-shaped funnels at the lower end.

Describe what happens. _____

_____

Try to explain your results. _____

_____

_____

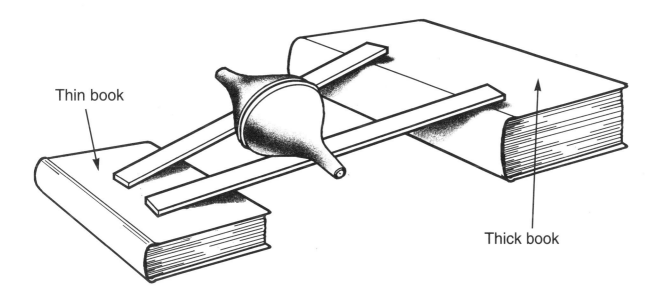

Thin book

Thick book

Newton Hint: Look at the funnel from the side with your eye level with the ramp.

Bug on a Wheel

Newton's Puzzler Description

A small bug is riding near the edge of a toy wheel. As the wheel rolls forward, the bug is taken along for the ride. The ride is not a simple one, because the bug is going forward as well as in a circular path.

What's the Problem?

What is the shape of the path that the bug follows as it travels both forward and around?

What Do You Think Will Happen?

What shape do you think the bug's path will be? Newton tried to outsmart this puzzle by riding around on one of the tires of his truck. Instead of finding an answer, he got dizzy.

On the back, sketch the path you think the bug on the wheel will take.

TLC10138 Copyright © Teaching & Learning Company, Carthage, IL 62321-0010

Name _____

How to Build Newton's Puzzler

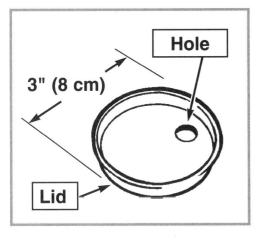

1. Obtain a round lid about 3" (8 cm) in diameter.

2. Punch a hole large enough for the point of a pen or pencil to go through near one edge.

3. Tape a ruler down on a tabletop.

4. Place a sheet of paper against the ruler.

5. Place the lid against the left end of the ruler.

6. Place the pen or pencil through the lid hole so that it marks the paper.

7. Use your thumb to roll the lid to the right along the ruler. Keep pressing on the pencil so it marks the paper as it simulates the bug's ride.

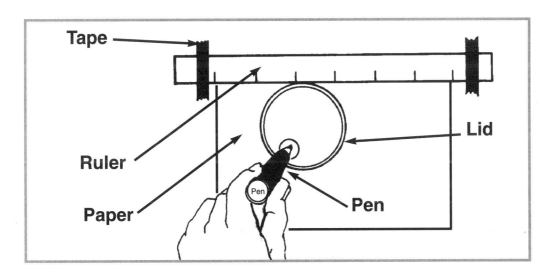

You might enjoy placing another hole in the lid halfway between the rim and the center of the lid. Do you think the path would be different than the bug near the rim? Newton would like to encourage you to try other ways of doing his puzzler.

TLC10138 Copyright © Teaching & Learning Company, Carthage, IL 62321-0010

Name _____

A Watery Puzzler

Newton's Puzzler Description

Newton's doctor ordered him to drink **exactly** four ounces (118 ml) of water at a time. He could not drink more. He could not drink less. He must drink exactly four ounces (118 ml).

What's the Problem?

Poor Newton had no measuring cup. He had telescopes and prisms and all kinds of scientific equipment. Newton had nothing in his lab to measure out the exact four ounces (118 ml) of water that he needed.

Newton did have paper cups. He had the five-ounce (148 ml) size. He had the three-ounce (89 ml) size. He had no four-ounce (118 ml) paper cups.

How Can Newton Solve This Puzzler?

Newton is very smart. He filled one of the cups to its capacity and then . . . ?

Can you figure out how Newton measured out exactly four ounces (118 ml) of water using only a three- and a five-ounce (89 and 148 ml) cup?

3 oz. cup   5 oz. cup

Describe your solution. You can use all the water you need to solve the problem.

_____

_____

_____

16

TLC10138 Copyright © Teaching & Learning Company, Carthage, IL 62321-0010

Bathroom Scale Puzzler

Newton's Puzzler Description

You are standing on a bathroom scale. Your arms are held straight out at your side. In condition A you flap your arms quickly upward in the air. In condition B you flap your arms quickly downward. Condition C is **imaginary**. You jump off the roof of a building with the scale strapped to your feet.

What's the Problem?

1. Will the scale read more, less or the same at the **instant** you raise your arms in condition A?

2. Will the scale read more, less or the same at the **instant** you lower your arms in condition A?

3. Assume you weigh 100 pounds (45 kg). Will the scale strapped to your feet read more, less or exactly 100 pounds (45 kg) as you are falling from the roof in condition C?

What Do You Think Will Happen?

Can you give a reasonable explanation for what you predicted in each of the three conditions?

Condition A: Give your prediction and explanation. _____

_____

_____

TLC10138 Copyright © Teaching & Learning Company, Carthage, IL 62321-0010

Name _____

Condition B: Give your prediction and explanation. _____

_____

_____

_____

Condition C: Give your prediction and explanation. _____

_____

_____

_____

How to Build Newton's Puzzler

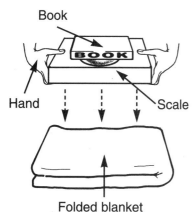

Book

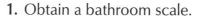

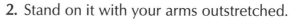

Hand

Scale

Folded blanket

1. Obtain a bathroom scale.

2. Stand on it with your arms outstretched.

3. Move them up **quickly** while observing the scale.

4. Move them down **quickly** from the outstretched position while observing the scale.

5. **Don't try condition C.** Newton thinks you and the bathroom scale are too valuable to science to risk jumping from a roof. Instead do your testing this way.

6. Place two heavy books on the top of the scale. Note their weight.

7. Hold the books and scale over a pad or folded blanket or pillow. This is an added precaution in case you can't catch the falling scale.

8. Keep your hands at the sides of the scale and allow the scale to fall for about 10" (25 cm). Your hands should be moving down with the scale to make it easier to catch.

9. Note the reading on the scale **during** falling.

18

TLC10138 Copyright © Teaching & Learning Company, Carthage, IL 62321-0010

The Mysterious Faucet

Newton's Puzzler Description

Study the drawing on the right. It shows water coming out of a faucet. The faucet is **not** connected to any water pipe. It is held in the air by two strings.

Magicians like to use this Newton puzzler to fool and amaze you. The faucet seems to have an unlimited supply of water.

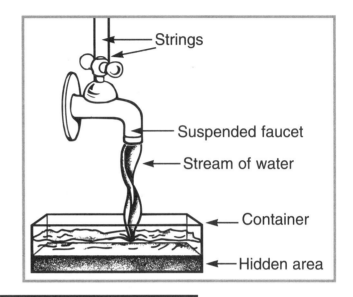

- Strings
- Suspended faucet
- Stream of water
- Container
- Hidden area

What's the Problem?

Where do you think the water is coming from? This is not magic. There is a scientific explanation. _____

_____

_____

_____

How to Build Newton's Puzzler

You'll have to first understand the secret behind this puzzler. You'll find the explanation and building instructions in the answer key.

TLC10138 Copyright © Teaching & Learning Company, Carthage, IL 62321-0010

Name _____

A Weighty Pulley

Newton's Puzzler Description

Two 500-gram weights are attached with string to **opposite** ends of a spring scale. Each string runs over a simple pulley as shown with the weights hanging down and in balance.

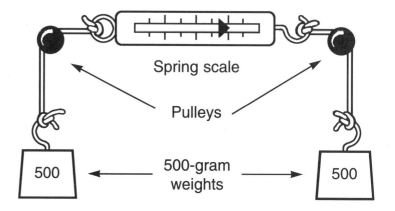

Spring scale

Pulleys

500   500-gram weights   500

What's the Problem?

What will be the reading in grams on the spring scale?

What Do You Think Will Happen?

Can you give a **reasonable** explanation for the weight you predict will be shown on the spring scale? _____

_____

_____

_____

20

TLC10138 Copyright © Teaching & Learning Company, Carthage, IL 62321-0010

Name _____

How to Build Newton's Puzzler

1. Obtain a spring scale, two 1-meter pieces of string and two 500-gram weights. You can use two equal books for weights if convenient.

2. Tie a string to each end of the spring scale.

3. Tie the other end of each string to a weight.

4. Drive two nails into a board about 30 centimeters apart. Leave part of the nails extending out of the wood. They will serve as simply pulleys.

5. Drape the strings over the pulleys and observe the reading on the spring scale as you hold the wood block.

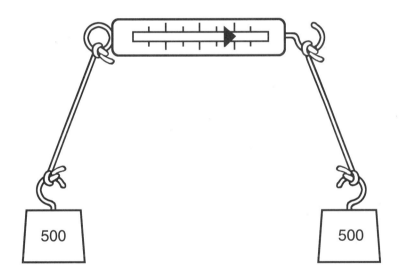

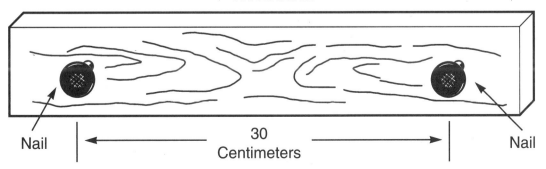

Wood block

Nail

30
Centimeters

Nail

How Square Is a Paper Cup?

Newton's Puzzler Description

So far in this puzzler book, you have not been asked to use the metric system. That is because most of you are more familiar with the American system of inches, pounds and quarts. Most scientists, and most people in the world, use the metric system.

This puzzler asks you to use a standard paper cup to make some metric measurements. You are going to try to find the number of square centimeters on the **outside surface** of a paper cup.

Below you will see a square centimeter marked off. It is one centimeter long on each side. For comparison, an inch is roughly equal to 2$^1/_2$ centimeters.

|1 cm|

What's the Problem?

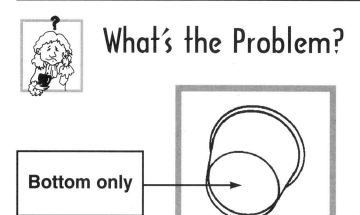

Bottom only

1. Can you find out how many centimeters of surface area are on the bottom of the cup?

TLC10138 Copyright © Teaching & Learning Company, Carthage, IL 62321-0010

Name _____

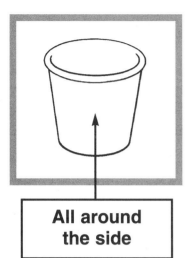

All around the side

2. Can you find out how many square centimeters of surface area are on the side of the cup? **Do not include the bottom area.**

3. Try to **estimate** the square centimeters first, before actually measuring the cup.

Your cup bottom estimate is _____ square centimeters.

Your cup side estimate is _____ square centimeters.

How to Solve Newton's Puzzler

1. Obtain a few standard kitchen size paper cups. They are the size that can hold about 148 milliliters of water. For you non-metrics, that is about four-fifths of a cup.

2. Use any method you wish to find the areas of the bottom and side of the cup.

Newton feels that you might need some hints. He suggests you consider cutting out the bottom of the cup. You can also make one cut down the side of the cup so that you can flatten it out. Are there any mathematical formulas you might use to help out? Scientists often solve science problems mathematically without even doing experiments.

Your cup bottom measurement is _____ square centimeters.

Your cup side measurement is _____ square centimeters.

The Center of Gravity

Newton Explains the Center of Gravity

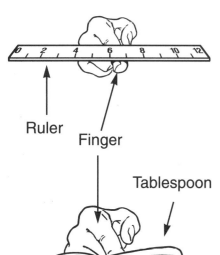

Ruler

Finger

Tablespoon

Balance a 12" (30 cm) ruler by placing your finger under the 6" (15 cm) mark. The ruler balances because equal weights are on both sides of your finger. The 6" (15 cm) point is the ruler's center of gravity because there are equal weights on both sides. Your ruler will not balance with your finger at the 5" (13 cm) mark.

Now let's find the center of balance of an irregular-shaped object.

1. Obtain a tablespoon.

2. Adjust your finger to find the point where the tablespoon balances. This is the spoon's center of gravity. Are there equal

   weights on both sides of your finger? _____ You also have a center of gravity. If you lean over too far, you will fall.

The Center of Gravity Problem

You have an irregular-shaped piece of cardboard. How can you find its center of gravity?

Think! What can you do to find the exact center of gravity of your cardboard? That would be the only point at which you could balance it with your finger. List your ideas below.

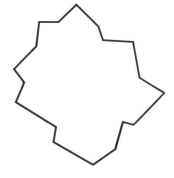

_____

_____

_____

_____

TLC10138 Copyright © Teaching & Learning Company, Carthage, IL 62321-0010

Name _____

How to Solve This Puzzler

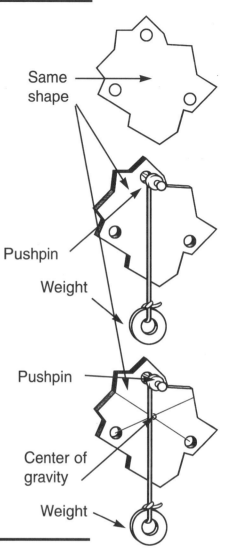

Same shape →

Pushpin

Weight

Pushpin

Center of gravity

Weight

1. Cut out an irregular shape from a piece of cardboard at least 8" x 11" (20 x 28 cm). Manila folders work fine.

2. Punch three holes with a paper punch at different points on the **edge** of your cardboard.

3. Obtain a pushpin, a piece of string and any small object to use as a weight.

4. Tie one end of the string to the weight.

5. Tie the other end to the pushpin.

6. Push the pin through one of the holes into a bulletin board or any convenient place. The cardboard, string and weight should swing freely.

7. Draw a line along the string.

8. Repeat for the other two holes.

9. You now have three different lines. Where they intersect is the cardboard's center of gravity.

10. Try to balance the irregular cardboard by placing your finger at the center of gravity.

Newton's Easier Method to Find the Center of Gravity

1. Use the unmarked side of your cardboard from the above activity.

2. Place your cardboard slightly over the edge of a table. Move it slowly toward the edge.

3. Draw a line where your cardboard just begins to fall over the edge.

4. Rotate your cardboard 90° and repeat the above. Your center of gravity is where your two lines cross.

5. Try balancing it with your finger at that point.

6. Compare it to the center of gravity you found on the reverse side of the cardboard using strings and weights. They should be almost the same.

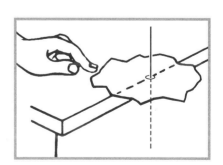

Name _____

Coffee Can Race

Newton's Puzzler Description

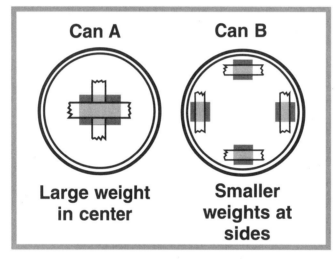

Can A

Can B

Large weight in center

Smaller weights at sides

You have two similar one-pound (.45 kg) coffee cans. Can A has one large weight taped to the center of the bottom. Can B has the same amount of weight. However, the weights are distributed differently. Can B has four smaller weights taped on opposite sides as shown. The four smaller weights roughly add up to the one larger weight on can A. Thus the total weight in both cans is about the same. The only difference is where the weights are located.

Both cans are started down a tilted table from the **same height** at the **same time.**

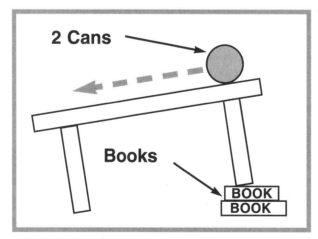

2 Cans

Books

BOOK
BOOK

What's the Problem?

Will can A roll downhill faster than can B? Or will can B roll faster?

TLC10138 Copyright © Teaching & Learning Company, Carthage, IL 62321-0010

Name _____

What Do You Think Will Happen?

Before you make your prediction, Newton wants to warn you that there may be another alternative. Could something else happen besides A beating B or B beating A? Scientists must be on the lookout for all kinds of possibilities. What is

your prediction? _____

_____

How to Build Newton's Puzzler

1. Obtain two coffee cans, one pound (.45 kg) in size.

2. Obtain weights. If available, use one 200-gram and four 50-gram weights borrowed from a science teacher. Otherwise, use lead fishing weights.

3. Tape the large weight to the **center** of the **bottom** of one coffee can.

4. Tape the four smaller weights to the **opposite sides** of the other can. For best balance, the four weights should be separated as close to 90° as possible.

5. Place books under both legs of **one** side of a long table to raise it about 4" (10 cm).

6. Line up coffee cans evenly at the high end of the table for the race. Let them go at the same time.

7. Have someone catch them as they get near the lower end.

8. It might be a good idea to repeat the race a few times to be sure you get consistent results.

9. It might help the cans to roll more evenly if you placed plastic coffee can lids on **both** ends of each can.

10. Describe the results and try to give an explanation. _____

_____

_____

Which Way Will I Blow?

Newton's Puzzler Description

Two light balls are suspended from a ruler. They are about a 1/4" (.6 cm) apart. Air blown through a straw is aimed between them.

What's the Problem?

What will happen to the two balls when a stream of air is blown between them?

What Do You Think Will Happen?

Will the balls be blown apart? Will they move closer together? Or will they remain where they started? Explain what you think will happen. _____

_____

28

TLC10138 Copyright © Teaching & Learning Company, Carthage, IL 62321-0010

Name _____

How to Build Newton's Puzzler

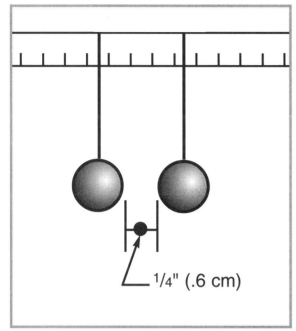

1/4" (.6 cm)

1. Obtain two Ping-Pong™ or other light balls.

2. Tape light string on each. For soft balls, such as Styrofoam™, simply push a pin into the ball.

3. Tie the other end of the string to a ruler or convenient stick.

4. Adjust the balls so they are hanging the **same** length and about 1/4" (.6 cm) apart.

5. Use a straw to blow a **gentle** stream of air between the balls.

Describe what happened. _____

_____

_____

_____

Would you believe that the science involved in this puzzler helps an airplane stay up in the air? Newton recommends that you look up Bernoulli's law in an encyclopedia and find out how Bernoulli's discoveries explain the ball's motion.

Name _____

Light Puzzlers

Newton's Coin Illusion

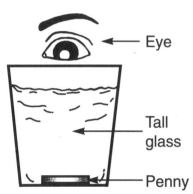

Eye

Tall glass

Penny

A penny is dropped into a tall glass of water. You are looking at the underwater penny from above the glass.

Here are your puzzler choices. Does the coin **appear** to be:

   a. as deep as it really is?

   b. deeper than it really is?

   c. nearer the surface than it really is?

1. Drop a penny into a tall glass of water.

2. Observe the coin from the top and side. Is your decision A, B or C? _____

How Big Is My Egg?

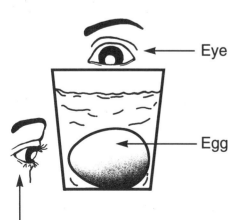

Eye

Egg

Eye

An egg is placed in a large glass of water. You can look at the egg from the top or side of the glass.

Here are your puzzler choices. Does the egg appear to be:

   a. its normal size?

   b. larger than normal size?

   c. smaller than normal size?

1. Carefully drop an egg into a tall glass of water.

2. Observe the egg from any angle. Is your decision A, B or C? _____

TLC10138 Copyright © Teaching & Learning Company, Carthage, IL 62321-0010

Name _____

Fishing for Dinner

You are on a tropical island. You decide to catch a fish for dinner. You walk into the ocean, look down and see a fish right in front of you. Here are your puzzler choices. To catch the fish, do you:

    a. reach where the fish appears to be?

    b. reach between you and where the fish appears?

    c. reach beyond where the fish appears?

1. Try to set up a large, deep, flat pan.

2. Use any 2" or 3" (5 or 8 cm) colorful object to be the fish.

3. Try to grab the fish. Was A, B or C correct?

_____

Building a Kaleidoscope

A kaleidoscope is a device using two mirrors to see colors and designs. Here's how to make a simple kaleidoscope.

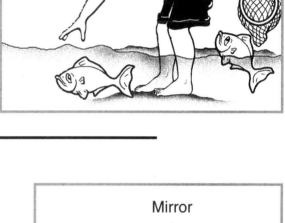

Mirror

1. Obtain two mirrors about 1" (2.5 cm) wide and 4" to 6" (10 to 15 cm) long. However, most any mirrors will work.

2. Tape the two mirrors together the long way.

3. Cut some black cardboard about the same length and width of your mirrors.

4. Use the black cardboard to finish a triangle. Tape the mirrors and cardboard securely.

5. Look through your kaleidoscope at colorful objects such as a stamp. Rotate the object for best effect.

Newton Hint: You can improve your kaleidoscope by covering the viewing end with cardboard and making a small opening for your eye. Adjusting the mirror angle can help. They are usually set at a 30° angle.

Name _____

The Slippery Yardstick

Newton's Puzzler Description

Place a finger at each end of a yard or meterstick. Hold the stick level. Move your fingers **slowly** toward the center of the stick.

What's the Problem?

Can you move one finger toward the center **without** moving the other finger?

Where on the stick will your fingers meet? _____

What Do You Think Will Happen?

Predict what will happen and try to explain your prediction. _____

_____

_____

What Happened When You Tried This Puzzler?

_____

_____

Newton Puzzler Extra: You've found out what happens when you start with your fingers at the ends and move in. What will happen when you **start** with both fingers at the **center** and move outward?

TLC10138 Copyright © Teaching & Learning Company, Carthage, IL 62321-0010

Arrow in a Tree

Newton's Puzzler Description

**3'
(.90 m)**

Newton lived on a farm when he was your age. Of course, that was so long ago that people used bows and arrows instead of guns. Newton once shot an arrow so deep into a young oak tree that no one could pull the arrow out.

This particular oak tree grew about 4' (1.2 m) every year. The arrow entered the tree just 3' (.90 m) above ground level.

What's the Problem?

Newton left the farm 10 years after he originally shot the arrow into the tree. How high was the arrow above ground after 10 years of tree growth? Write your prediction below.

_____

_____

_____

_____

TLC10138 Copyright © Teaching & Learning Company, Carthage, IL 62321-0010

Name _____

How to Test Newton's Puzzler

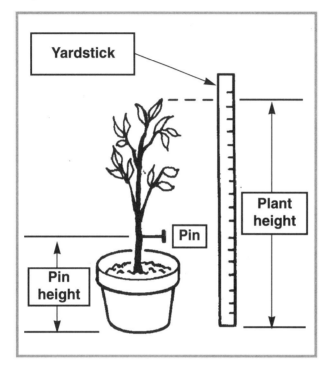

You could shoot an arrow into a tree and wait 10 years. But there is a faster way to test this puzzler.

1. Obtain a fast-growing young plant.

2. Measure from the bottom of the container and record its height. _____ inches (cm)

3. Stick a small pin into the stem to represent the arrow.

4. Measure the distance in inches (centimeters) from the pin to the bottom of the container. _____ inches (cm)

5. Wait eight to 10 days. Remeasure both the plant's height and the pin's height.

Plant height: _____ inches (cm)   Pin height: _____ inches (cm)

Be patient. Wait the eight to 10 days before looking up the answer. Newton studied the planets' motions for years before he developed laws about their orbits. New discoveries in science are not made instantly.

TLC10138 Copyright © Teaching & Learning Company, Carthage, IL 62321-0010

The Balancing Stick

Newton's Puzzler Description

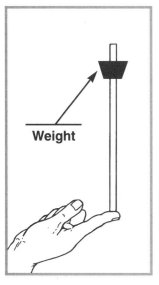

Weight

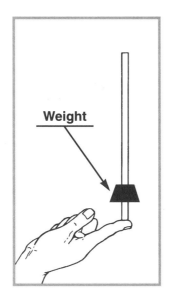

Weight

A long stick is placed through a weight as shown in the diagram. Notice that the stick extends about 1" (2.5 cm) through the weight. The end of the stick is balanced on the tip of **one** finger. The device will be balanced first with the weight up and then with the weight down.

What's the Problem?

Will the stick balance better with the weight **up** or **down**? Or will they balance the same either way?

What Do You Think Will Happen?

Can you give a reasonable explanation for your prediction? Perhaps you've had some everyday experience that you can relate to this balancing problem.

_____

_____

TLC10138 Copyright © Teaching & Learning Company, Carthage, IL 62321-0010

How to Build Newton's Puzzler

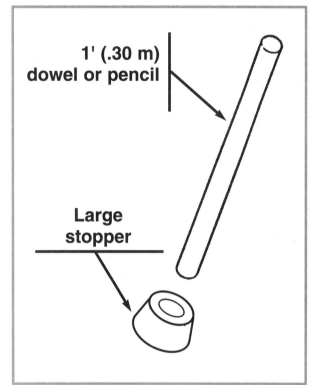

1' (.30 m) dowel or pencil

Large stopper

Obtain a round stick (often called a dowel) about $1/4$" (.6 cm) in diameter and at least 1' (.30 m) long. A new pencil can be used as a substitute. You will also need a large one-hole rubber stopper.

1. **Carefully** insert the stick into the stopper so that it extends out about 1" (2.5 cm). Place soapy water on the dowel to help.

2. Try balancing the stick a few times the way you predicted that it would balance best.

3. Now try balancing it a few times the opposite way.

Describe your results. _____

_____

_____

_____

Sometimes people come to conclusions based upon prejudice. Just because you predicted a particular outcome, doesn't mean an experiment will turn out that way. Newton encourages you to keep an open mind. This is important in both science and real life.

TLC10138 Copyright © Teaching & Learning Company, Carthage, IL 62321-0010

Perpetual Motion

Newton's Puzzler Description

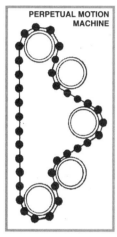

PERPETUAL MOTION MACHINE

A perpetual motion machine is like something for nothing. It is a device that can do work but does not require you to put in any energy.

No one has ever succeeded in building a perpetual motion machine. Almost all scientists believe that it is impossible to build one because it goes against the basic laws of energy.

In the true spirit of science, Newton has attempted to build three perpetual motion devices. They are shown and explained below and on the following page.

What's the Problem?

Can you explain why Newton's three perpetual motion devices will not work?

What Do You Think Will Happen?

Perpetual Motion Device No. 1–The Downhill Car

Newton built a car with huge back wheels and tiny front wheels. It is always running downhill.

1. Why won't the downhill car work? _____

_____

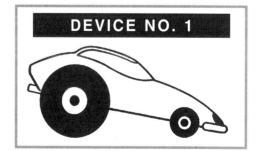

DEVICE NO. 1

TLC10138 Copyright © Teaching & Learning Company, Carthage, IL 62321-0010

Name _____

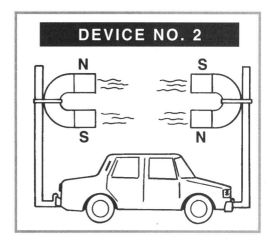

Perpetual Motion Device No. 2–The Magnetic Car

Newton mounted a powerful horseshoe magnet above the front bumper of his car. He mounted another powerful magnet above the rear bumper. He faced the magnets so they attracted each other. As the front magnet pulled on the rear magnet, the car zoomed forward.

2. Why won't the magnetic car work? _____

_____

_____

_____

Perpetual Motion Device No. 3–The Motor Generator

A generator produces electrical energy that can drive a motor. The generator requires some form of energy to turn its shaft so that it can work.

If a motor is supplied electrical energy from a generator, its shaft will spin. Newton simply attached

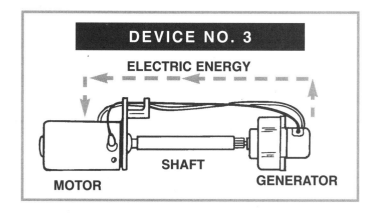

this spinning shaft to the generator. He fed the generator's electricity back to the motor. He thought he had a perpetual motion device because no outside energy was used to make the device work.

3. Why won't the motor generator work? _____

_____

_____

Newton knows that it is impossible to build a perpetual motion machine. Two laws of energy explain how machines work. The first law says that energy cannot be created or destroyed. The second says that heat, which is a form of energy, can only flow from a hot object to a cold object. No machine ever built created more energy than it used.

38

The Candle Snuffer

Newton's Puzzler Description

Our helpful friend Newton is very old. Actually he was born in the year 1642. Thomas Edison hadn't invented the light bulb yet. Newton read and worked using candles. To put candles out, people used a **candle snuffer**.

This puzzler is about a different kind of snuffer. It appears to turn a candle flame off and then on again.

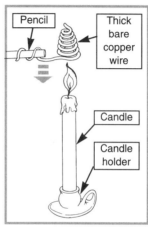

Pencil

Thick bare copper wire

Candle

Candle holder

What's the Problem?

You won't understand the problem until you actually observe the snuffer in action. You'll be told the problem after you have built your candle snuffer.

How to Build Newton's Puzzler

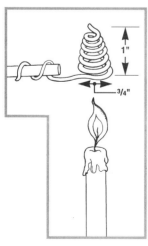

1"

3/4"

1. Obtain about 16" (41 cm) of stiff, bare (uninsulated) copper wire. The thicker the wire's diameter, the better.

2. Roll it into a cone shape. The outside diameter of the *bottom* of the cone can be about 3/4" (1.9 cm). The height of the cone should be about 1" (2.5 cm). About eight to 10 turns should be made with small spaces between each turn. See the sketch on the left for help.

Name _____

3. Wrap the other end of the copper wire on one end of a pencil. This will serve as a handle.

4. Place a large candle in a secure base. Do not use a birthday candle.

5. Light the candle. Think **safety** with the candle.

6. Lower your snuffer directly over the flame as shown. **Do not touch the candle itself.** Leave it for a very few seconds, and then **quickly** raise the snuffer at least 1' (.30 m) above the flame.

7. Allow the candle snuffer to **cool for one minute**, and then try it again.

8. Repeat a few more times and observe carefully.

9. What happened as you lowered the candle snuffer? _____

_____

_____

_____

10. What happened when you quickly raised the candle snuffer?_____

_____

_____

_____

11. Can you explain how a candle that apparently goes out can relight itself?

_____

_____

_____

Newton included this puzzler to help you improve your powers of observation. If this puzzler puzzles you, perhaps you did not do a good job of observing. Before looking up the answer, Newton suggests that you repeat the experiment in a darkened room. Perhaps you can observe something in the dark that you hadn't observed before.

TLC10138 Copyright © Teaching & Learning Company, Carthage, IL 62321-0010

The Candle Snuffer Puzzler

Newton Explains the Candle Snuffer Contest

As of now, it is against the law to blow out a candle. Your class has been selected to solve the awesome problem of finding alternate ways to snuff out candles.

The new law requires that candles cannot be snuffed out directly. That would be cruel. Your candle snuffer must have at least two and no more than four stages. For example, a falling weight could release a can that would fall on top of and smother the candle.

Your team will be given planning time to solve this problem. Some of the devices may have to be built at home.

All proposed candle snuffers must be *neatly sketched* and submitted in advance to your teacher **before they are built**. Your teacher will check for **safety**, decide whether it has a chance of working and give you a few helpful suggestions.

You will have an opportunity to present your candle snuffer to the class.

Judging the Candle Snuffer Contest

1. Your invention will be judged on workmanship. It must be sturdily built.

2. Your invention and chart must be neat and colorful.

3. Your invention will be judged on how well it works.

4. You can win bonus points by originality. Try to build your candle snuffer differently from the other entries.

5. The more stages (up to four) you have, the more bonus points you can earn.

6. You can earn bonus points for unique applications of basic scientific principles.

Newton Help: The **candle snuffer problem** is basically a classical Rube Goldberg device where one motion or activity precipitates another. There is no limit to the possibilities. Objects can roll down ramps or springs can release devices. Chemical reactions such as vinegar and baking soda could generate carbon dioxide.

Allow adequate time between planning and class demonstrations. In all cases you supply and light the candles. If time is limited, each team can skip construction and just plan, sketch and give oral reports.

Name _____

Those Crazy Mixed-Up Eggs

Newton's Puzzler Description

Newton loves to experiment. A few years ago he developed a new kind of chicken that laid only **hard-boiled eggs**. His experiments were a great success until the day his wife left the gate open. His prize chickens escaped and got all mixed up with the normal chickens that laid normal **raw** eggs.

What's the Problem?

When Newton's wife collected the eggs from the mixed-up chickens, she couldn't tell which were hard-boiled and which were raw. But scientist Newton had no trouble separating the hard-boiled from the raw eggs. Can you find at least four ways to separate them **without breaking the shells**?

What Do You Think Will Happen?

Before trying any egg experiments, list four methods that you predict will work. Remember that your methods cannot harm the eggs or even break the shell.

1. _____

2. _____

42

TLC10138 Copyright © Teaching & Learning Company, Carthage, IL 62321-0010

Name _____

3. _____

4. _____

Newton wants you to know that what you are doing is called **hypothesizing**. When you hypothesize about eggs or anything else, you are really making an educated guess. Your guess can be right or wrong. You won't know until you test your hypothesis. Hypothesizing is a difficult but important part of the scientific process.

How to Solve Newton's Puzzler

There is nothing to build. To insure that the egg tests are fair, have a friend, teacher or parent pick out four similar eggs. They should boil only two. Place no markings on the eggs and mix them up. Now go to work testing.

Which of your tests worked? _____

_____

_____

Which new ways of identifying the eggs did you discover? _____

_____

_____

You'll notice that in this puzzler you were given a problem and practically no help in solving the problem. Actually there are many solutions to this egg problem just as scientists find many solutions to their scientific problems. Newton found four solutions to the egg problem. Newton's wife found six solutions. How many can you find?

TLC10138 Copyright © Teaching & Learning Company, Carthage, IL 62321-0010

Name _____

The Falling Target

Newton's Puzzler Description

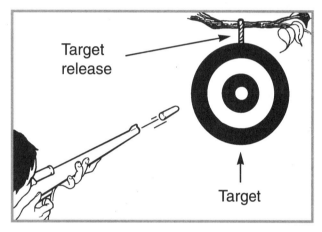

Target release

Target

There once was an Olympic rifle marksman who wanted to improve his marksmanship. He hooked up a target that would fall **exactly** when the bullet left his rifle.

He took aim at the target from a distance of 50 yards (46 m). That is one half the length of a football field. As he had planned, the target began to drop at the exact moment that the bullet left the rifle.

What's the Problem?

Assume the bullet left the rifle at the very instant the target dropped from the tree. Will the bullet strike the target or fly over or under the target?

How to Test Newton's Puzzler

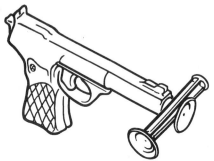

1. Obtain a toy dart gun and two arrows.

2. Place one dart into the gun. This takes the place of the bullet.

3. Place the other dart as shown pressed between the first dart and the gun's opening. This takes the place of the falling target.

TLC10138 Copyright © Teaching & Learning Company, Carthage, IL 62321-0010

Name _____

4. **Safely** aim the gun at a wide open space.

5. Hold the gun as horizontally as you can.

6. Fire the dart gun.

7. Use your eyes or a friend's eyes to determine how the darts fell.

8. Better still, use your ears. Your ears can tell if the darts hit the ground together or separately.

Describe what happened. _____

_____

Newton's testing device uses toy darts to represent both the bullet and the target. Scientists often are not able to solve their problems directly and must use some substitutions in their experiment. Could you think of another indirect way of testing this rifle and target puzzle?

Newton and Galileo Get Together

Newton studied gravity. He became interested when an apple fell out of a tree and hit him. Galileo supposedly dropped different size cannonballs from the Leaning Tower of Pisa.

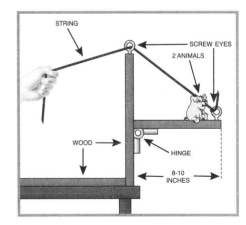

Let's combine Newton and Galileo's experiments by building the device shown on the right. You will be comparing the falling rate of heavy and light objects. The device insures that both stuffed animals drop at the same time.

1. Obtain two small stuffed animals about the same size.

2. Fill one of the stuffed animals with nails, nuts and bolts so that it is much heavier than the other.

3. Assemble the dropping device. You will need some wood, a hinge, two screw eyes and some string.

Based upon your dropping experiment, which fell faster? _____

_____

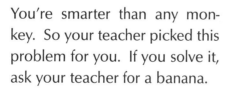

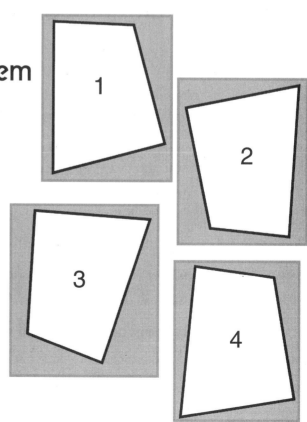

Name _____

Solving Problems Puzzler

Everybody Has Problems

Scientists solve problems. Their problems are about space, medicine, gravity or weather.

Even animals can solve problems. In a science experiment, a monkey was placed in a room. Some bananas were hanging from the ceiling. The scientist left a box in the corner. First the monkey tried to jump up to grab the bananas. He failed because they were hanging too high.

Can you guess how the monkey solved his problem? He pushed the box under the bananas, climbed up and enjoyed his feast.

The Perfect Square Problem

You're smarter than any monkey. So your teacher picked this problem for you. If you solve it, ask your teacher for a banana.

Cut out the four figures shown below. They might be easier to work with if you traced them on cardboard. All four are exactly alike.

Can you put them together to make a *perfect square*? A perfect square has all sides the same and all corners make right angles. There cannot be a hole in the center.

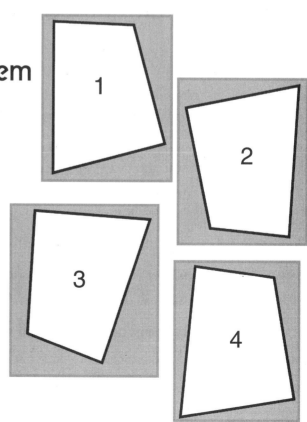

1

2

3

4

46

Brain Puzzlers–No Equipment Needed

Newton's Puzzler Description

E=MC²

Newton would have admired Albert Einstein. Einstein was able to solve many science problems using only his brain. There were no computers in his day. Einstein's tools were pencil and paper or chalk and a chalkboard. His famous equation $E = MC^2$ explained how energy and matter are related.

The following brain puzzlers require no tools and no construction. They can all be done in your head.

Find the Counterfeit Silver Dollar

Newton was given nine silver dollars that looked and felt the same. He was told that one of the dollars was counterfeit and weighed a bit **less**. The other eight were real.

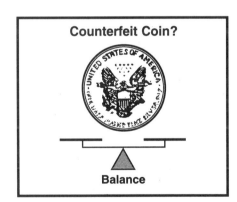

Counterfeit Coin?

Balance

1. Newton had a balance available.

2. He could only use it **two** times.

3. How did Newton discover which was the lighter counterfeit coin in just **two** weighings?

4. Describe how you would solve this problem. Newton wants to give you a hint.

   You will have to weigh the coins a few at a time. _____

   _____

   _____

   _____

   _____

TLC10138 Copyright © Teaching & Learning Company, Carthage, IL 62321-0010

Name _____

The Impossible Coin

Archaeologists were digging at the site of an ancient Egyptian city. They found a gold coin marked *300 B.C.* on its face. How did they know that the gold coin was a fake?

Newton's Triangle Puzzle

Some people considered Newton a square. Those who knew him and loved him thought he was more of a triangle.

How many triangles can you find in the diagram below? _____ triangles

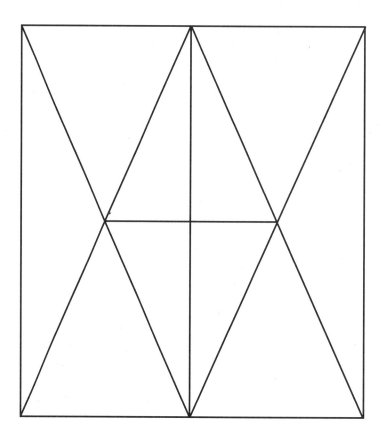

TLC10138 Copyright © Teaching & Learning Company, Carthage, IL 62321-0010

Name _____

More Puzzling Puzzlers

The Falling Stick Race

Obtain a 12" (30 cm) ruler and a 36" (91 cm) yardstick. Hold them both vertically as shown. Use one finger on each to hold them both **vertical**.

1. What do you predict will happen when you release both fingers at the same time allowing the sticks to

   fall? Which will hit the ground first? _____

   _____

   _____

   _____

2. Now release both fingers at the **same** time. Describe what happened.

   _____

   _____

   _____

Can you explain what happened? _____

_____

_____

_____

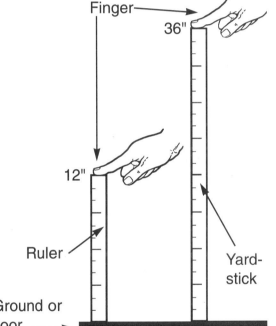

Finger

36"

12"

Ruler

Yard-stick

Ground or floor →

TLC10138 Copyright © Teaching & Learning Company, Carthage, IL 62321-0010

Name _____

Ping-Pong™ Puzzler

Obtain a Ping-Pong™ (or other light ball) and a wide-mouth small jar.

1. Place the ball inside the jar on a table.

2. Place a heavy science book upright as shown.

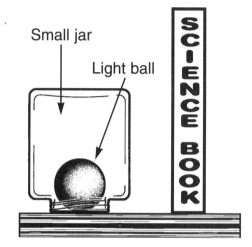

Small jar

Light ball

SCIENCE BOOK

Here is your problem. You must move the **ball and the jar** up and over the upright book. You can touch the jar, but you **cannot touch the ball**.

Think about the problem **before** trying the experiment. How do you propose to solve this puzzler? _____

_____

_____

Now try to solve the problem. **Be careful** with the glass jar.

50

TLC10138 Copyright © Teaching & Learning Company, Carthage, IL 62321-0010

I'm Falling for You

Newton's Puzzler Description

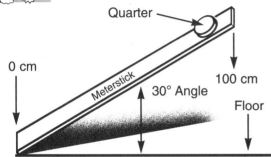

Quarter

0 cm

Meterstick

100 cm

30° Angle

Floor

The zero end of a meterstick is placed on the floor. The 100-centimeter end is tilted at **roughly** a 30° angle. A quarter is placed at the high end. You release the high end and let the quarter fall.

What's the Problem?

Will the quarter stay with the meterstick as it falls, or will the quarter drop more slowly and partially leave the meterstick?

What Do You Think Will Happen?

Describe what you think will happen and try to explain why. _____

_____

_____

_____

_____

TLC10138 Copyright © Teaching & Learning Company, Carthage, IL 62321-0010

Name _____

How to Build Newton's Puzzler

1. Tape three quarters together to add to their weight. You could use one or two checkers instead.

2. Cut two pieces of straw the same width as your meterstick.

3. Tape your straw pieces at the 95- and 50-centimeter points. The straws are to act as a ledge to hold the quarters in place.

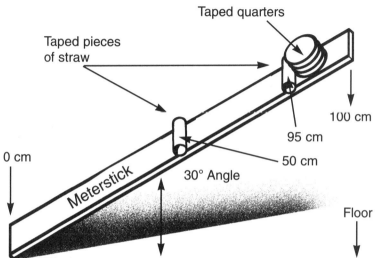

4. Place the quarters at the top end, adjust the meterstick to approximately 30° and let it go.

5. Observe the quarters and meterstick carefully as you repeat the experiment a few times.

Newton Extra: You taped a straw ledge at the 50-centimeter mark. Place the quarters on this ledge and repeat the experiment. Did the quarters fall with the meterstick or lag behind as it did at the 100-centimeter mark? Repeat the experiment a few times.

TLC10138 Copyright © Teaching & Learning Company, Carthage, IL 62321-0010

Name _____

Where Is My Penny?

Newton's Puzzler Description

Place a cereal bowl on a table. Place a penny in the center of the bowl. Walk backward facing the table and bowl. Keep walking backward until the penny disappears from your view.

What's the Problem?

You cannot see the penny from where you are standing. What **simple** thing can you do to make the penny visible? You cannot move. The bowl and penny cannot be touched or moved.

How Do You Plan to Solve the Invisible Penny Problem?

First list two of your ideas below. Then try them out.

Solution 1: Describe your plan and how it worked. _____

_____

_____

_____

Solution 2: Describe your plan and how it worked. _____

_____

_____

_____

TLC10138 Copyright © Teaching & Learning Company, Carthage, IL 62321-0010

Name _____

The Floating Candle

Newton's Puzzler Description

Study the diagram to the right. It shows a lit candle floating in water.

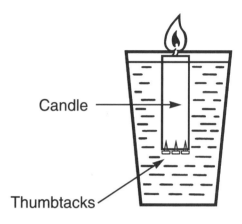

Candle

Thumbtacks

What's the Problem?

What will happen to the candle as it burns? Will it float upward, sink or remain at the same height above the water?

How Will You Solve This Puzzler?

Give your guess and reasons for your guess. _____

_____

_____

_____

_____

TLC10138 Copyright © Teaching & Learning Company, Carthage, IL 62321-0010

Name _____

How to Test This Newton Puzzler

1. Obtain a kitchen candle. Do not use a birthday candle.

2. Obtain a tall, thin jar or glass. An olive jar or a graduated cylinder works fine.

3. Fill your jar with water to within 1" (2.5 cm) of the top.

4. Push a few thumbtacks into the candle bottom. You want to weight the candle so that it floats upright as shown. Add or subtract thumbtacks until you get about $^1/_2$" (1.25 cm) of the candle extending above the water line. You also may have to add or subtract water.

5. **Carefully light the candle.** You may wish to obtain adult help.

6. Observe the candle as it burns.

Did the candle sink, float upward or remain at the same height? _____

_____

Roll, Roll, Roll Your Hoop

Newton's Puzzler Description

You have a cardboard hoop. You have a straw. Using the setup on the right, you can easily make the hoop roll forward.

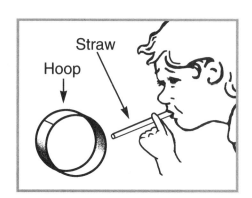

Straw

Hoop

What's the Problem?

How can you use your breath and your straw to make the hoop roll backward toward you?

How Will You Solve This Puzzler?

Sketch what you plan to do and tell how it should work. _____

_____

_____

_____

_____

TLC10138 Copyright © Teaching & Learning Company, Carthage, IL 62321-0010

Name _____

How to Build Newton's Puzzler

1. Cut a strip of cardboard **approximately** 11^1/$_2$" x 2^1/$_2$" (29 x 6 cm). Sections of manila folders work fine.

2. Use tape (not staples) to form it into a circular hoop.

Now try out your solution to the problem by blowing at the hoop through your straw.

Describe your results.

_____

_____

_____

Newton Contest: Once you have solved this puzzler (or checked the answer section), set up a contest. Find out who can make the hoop roll **backwards** the furthest with just **one** blow through the straw. Use a long table as your racetrack.

Predicting Circular Segments

Newton's Puzzler Description

Scientists think in terms of math. They measure distance, volume, weight and time. The data that scientists collect is usually arranged in tables and graphs. The data and graphs help them predict the results of an experiment. Sometimes their predictions are right. Sometimes their predictions are wrong.

In this puzzler, Newton is going to have you collect data and make predictions. You will need a sharp mind and a sharp pencil. How will **your** predictions turn out?

Drawing Newton's Circular Segments

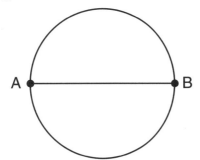

The circle to the left has two points (A and B) on its circumference. One line (AB) has been drawn between the points. This divides the circle into two spaces (the top and the bottom). Notice how the information about this circle has been placed on the data table on the next page.

Fill out the data table on the next page as you proceed. It will provide the basis for your later predictions.

TLC10138 Copyright © Teaching & Learning Company, Carthage, IL 62321-0010

Name _____

CIRCULAR SEGMENT DATA TABLE

Points on Circumference	Lines	Spaces
2	1	2
3		
4		
5		
6		

1. The circle to the right has three points on its circumference. Lines have been drawn between the three points. Count the number of lines and spaces and fill in the data table.

2. Repeat using the circle to the right with four points on its circumference. **Be sure *every* point is connected to *every* other point with a line**. Fill in the data table.

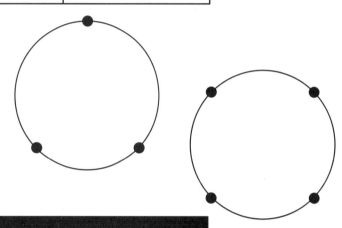

Prediction Time: Don't draw any lines on the next circle until you have followed the instructions and made your predictions.

3. Take a good look at your data table. You should see a pattern that will enable you to predict the number of lines and spaces for a circle with five points. For example, take the number series 1, 3, 5, ___. Since each increases by two, the blank space should be 7. On the number series 1, 3, 9, ___, the numbers are all multiplied by 3, so the blank space is 27.

4. Using the data table **only** try to predict the number of lines and spaces for the circle with five points. Fill in your predictions below **before** drawing lines.

Predicted number of lines with five points: _____

Predicted number of spaces with five points: _____

5. Now draw **all** possible lines on your five-pointed circle.

6. Count the lines and spaces and record them in the data table. Your prediction should match your real count. Go back and check if they are not the same.

TLC10138 Copyright © Teaching & Learning Company, Carthage, IL 62321-0010

Name _____

Frustration Time

Now you have a circle with six points. Repeat what you did on the preceding page by trying to predict the number of lines and spaces. Do this **before** you actually draw all possible lines between your six points.

Predicted number of lines:

_____

Predicted number of spaces:

_____

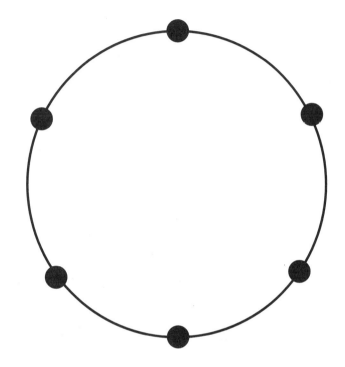

1. Now draw all possible lines between your six points.

2. Count the lines and spaces and record them in your data table.

3. Compare your predicted and actual lines and spaces and get frustrated.

Newton is also frustrated. His predictions did not match up with his real lines and spaces. Check your lines and spaces again for possible mistakes. In real science, predictions and experiments don't always match. Scientists learn from their mistakes.

TLC10138 Copyright © Teaching & Learning Company, Carthage, IL 62321-0010

Answer Key

How to Build Newton's Puzzler, page 6

If you did everything correctly, your yardstick rolled forward exactly twice the can's circumference. The can rolled one circumference distance along the table. Because the yardstick was not attached to the can, it rolled another circumference along the top of the can.

Newton Lost His Balloon, page 7

The balloon will expand as it rises. The dense air inside the balloon will push outward against the high thin air.

Balloon in a Bottle, page 7

You can blow up a balloon in a bottle if you find a way of letting the bottle's trapped air escape. Place a straw between the balloon and the bottle to help the air escape.

Balloon Blowing Competition, page 8

Some simple ways are by using vinegar and baking soda, also seltzer, sugar solution and yeast, dry ice or heating a flask with a balloon attached.

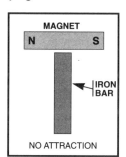

Magnetic Mystery, page 9

To solve this puzzler, you must know the nature of a magnet. A magnet has a North and South pole. The magnetic force is greatest at the poles and a minimum at the magnet's center. If you place either the North or South pole of the real magnet anywhere on the iron bar, you will feel attraction. If you place the end of the iron bar in the center of the magnet, there will be little or no attraction.

Optical Decisions, page 10

1. Circle number 5 matches.
2. Line C continues.

Can Lines Fool You? page 11

Lines A and B are unequal on optical illusions numbers 1 and 5.

How to Build Newton's Puzzler, page 13

The double cone only appears to go upward because the ramp widens. The actual center of gravity at the taped rims.

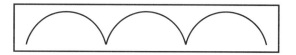

How to Build Newton's Puzzler, page 15

You've learned that the bug does not go in a circle. The bug's path is roughly like the path below.

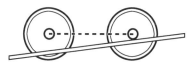

A Watery Puzzler, page 16

Fill the three-ounce (89 ml) cup with water. Pour the three ounces into the five-ounce (148 ml) cup. Fill the three-ounce cup again with water. Use it to fill the five-ounce cup to the brim. That took two ounces (59 ml) of water and left one ounce (29 ml) of water in the three-ounce cup. Pour out *all* the water in the five-ounce cup. Pour the one ounce of water into the five-ounce cup. Refill the three-ounce cup and pour the three ounces of water into the five-ounce cup. You now have exactly the four ounces of water that Newton needed.

Bathroom Scale Puzzler, pages 17-18

Newton's law of action and reaction explains conditions A and B. When your arms went up rapidly, the weight reading increased. When your arms went down rapidly, the weight reading decreased.

When your arms flew up, the body received a downward reaction causing the scale to go up. When you flapped the arms down, the opposite reaction on your body was up causing a decrease.

In condition C, the books and the scale are in free fall. There is essentially no downward pressure on the scale, and it should read close to zero.

How to Build Newton's Puzzler, page 19

This is an old magic trick. The water does not originate in the suspended faucet. There is a small water

Answer Key

pump in the mystery area. The pump pushes water *up* through a glass or plastic tube. The water falls back down on the *outside* of the tube. This gives the illusion of a water stream. You don't need a water pump. Build this in a sink. Connect rubber tubing from the sink to the glass tube. Use leaves and stones to hide the tubing.

What Do You Think Will Happen? page 20

The spring scale will read 500 grams. One 500-gram weight extends the scales to 500. The other merely acts as a support to hold the scale up. Its effect is the same as if you had nailed the top of the spring scale to the wall. The pulleys as used here do not change anything. They simply serve to change the pull's direction.

How to Solve Newton's Puzzler, page 23

Paper cups vary in size so there is no one answer. You could repeat the measurement on a similar cup to check your results. Have a friend do the same measurements and compare results.

Cut out the cup bottom and then cut through the rounded side. The bottom is a circle whose area is πr^2. The cup side **roughly** equals a trapezoid whose area can be found by adding the top and bottom and dividing the answer by two. Multiply that answer by the height and you have the area.

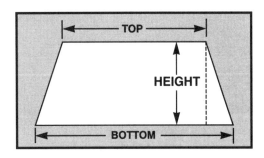

What Do You Think Will Happen? page 27

Can A with the center weight will beat can B. Understanding why is not easy. The physics of angular momentum, inertia and kinetic energy all enter into the explanation. You might want to check these physics concepts in an encyclopedia.

The analogy to an ice skater might help. When an ice skater wants to spin fast, he or she will bring their arms inward. When they want to slow their spinning,

they stretch their arms outward. They change their arm position to change their body weight distribution. They spin faster when the weight is centered. Your can with the weight centered also rolled down faster.

What Do You Think Will Happen? page 28

Blowing air between the suspended balls makes them move toward each other. The principle behind their action is called Bernoulli's Law. As air speeds up, the pressure goes down. You speeded up the air by blowing between the suspended balls. Therefore, the air between the balls had less than normal air pressure. The normal air pressure on the outside of the balls forced them inward.

Newton's Coin Illusion, page 30

The answer is C. Because of the bending of light as it moves from air to water, the coin will appear nearer the surface than it really is.

How Big Is My Egg? page 30

The answer is B. The water acts like a lens to magnify the egg.

Fishing for Dinner, page 31

The answer is B. The diagram shows how a light ray is bent as it leaves the water. Your eye is fooled into thinking the fish is further in front of you than it really is.

What Happened When You Tried This Puzzler? page 32

No matter how you try, both fingers will meet in the center. Friction is the reason. There is always some friction between your finger and the stick. Let's say one finger has slightly less friction and starts toward

TLC10138 Copyright © Teaching & Learning Company, Carthage, IL 62321-0010

Answer Key

the center. As it moves toward the center, it carries more of the stick's weight. This adds to the friction causing the other finger to move in. The fingers will take turns moving in until they meet. As you start at the center, the opposite happens. As any one finger moves outward, it supports less weight and has less friction. One finger will move to the end while the other remains centered.

Arrow in a Tree, pages 33-34

The arrow should be the same height above the ground at the end of 10 years. Trees and other plants grow from their tips. Trees can grow horizontally but that would only mean that the arrow is further from the tree's center.

The Balancing Stick, pages 35-36

The stick with the weight at the top is easier to balance. The top weight forms a longer arc as it falls, and you have more **time** to adjust to its fall. The bottom weight forms a shorter arc, and you do not have time to adjust.

The center of gravity for the weight and stick is a little above the weight. For balance purposes, the total weight is assumed to be at the center of gravity.

You can find the center of gravity by holding the weighted stick horizontal. Move your finger along until it balances.

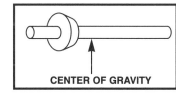

Perpetual Motion, pages 37-38

The downhill car still needs some form of energy to propel it forward. Assume you started it with a push. The friction of the wheels and air resistance will eventually slow it down.

The magnetic car will also go nowhere. The forces pulling the car are equal and opposite. They cancel out and the car remains motionless.

Electric generators and motors are similar. They both involve magnets, wires and motion. Motion results in friction, heat and a loss of energy. Both the motor and generator have friction energy losses. Assume the generator puts out 100 watts of energy to the motor. The 100 watts turn the motor shaft connected to the generator. Due to friction losses, the motor may only be supplying 80 watts of energy to the generator. That is not enough to sustain the original 100 watts of output.

The Candle Snuffer, pages 39-40

If done correctly, the candle will appear to go out and then relight itself. Any candle that was really out could not relight itself. If you observed carefully, especially in the dark, you would have seen a pale blue flame that never went out.

Here is what happens. The copper wire is an excellent conductor of heat. It cooled the burning gases down to a temperature where it burned light blue instead of the normal hot flame color.

Those Crazy Mixed-Up Eggs, pages 42-43

Here are four ways to find differences between raw and hard-boiled eggs.

1. Use a strong light. A raw egg is more transparent. A hard-boiled egg is more opaque.
2. Float both in salt water. The boiled eggs will tend to float higher than the raw eggs.
3. Try spinning both eggs. A hard-boiled egg will spin longer. The raw egg spins less because the liquid inside doesn't rotate as fast and acts to brake the spinning motion.
4. Spin a hard-boiled egg. Quickly stop and then release the egg. It will not move again. Now spin a raw egg. Quickly stop and release it. The liquid inside is still spinning, so the raw egg will continue to rotate.

How to Test Newton's Puzzler, pages 44-45

Gravity never takes a vacation. It acts the same on the speeding bullet as it does on the falling target. Since the bullet and the target drop the same vertical distance, they will hit the ground at the same time.

TLC10138 Copyright © Teaching & Learning Company, Carthage, IL 62321-0010

Answer Key

Newton and Galileo Get Together, page 45

The heavy and light stuffed animals fall at the same rate. If they were dropped from an airplane, the light animal would fall more slowly. That is due to the resistance of the air molecules. The animals dropped on the moon would always fall at the same rate. There are no air molecules on the moon.

The Perfect Square, page 46

Find the Counterfeit Silver Dollar, page 47

Divide the nine dollar coins into three groups of three. Place two of the groups on the balance, one group in each pan. This will reveal in which group the *light* dollar is. If the two groups on the balance both balance each other, the light dollar is in the third group. Balance two of the dollars from the "light" group, one in each pan of the balance. If they balance, the remaining dollar is the light or the counterfeit dollar.

The Impossible Coin, page 48

No coin created before the birth of Christ could be labeled *B.C.*, which stands for "Before Christ."

Newton's Triangle Puzzle, page 48

There are 24 triangles.

The Falling Stick Race, page 49

The ruler always falls first. Scientists like to assume all weight is in the object's *center*. For the ruler, that is at the 6" (15 cm) mark. For the yardstick, that is at the 18" (46 cm) mark. It takes longer to fall from 18" than 6".

Ping-Pong™ Puzzler, page 50

You have to have a very light ball and the correctly shaped jar for this to work. (See jar on page 50. Many baby food jars will work. The jar should have a short neck, at least three-fourths of the ball should extend above the neck.) Place your hand firmly on the jar and rotate both your hand and the jar in a circle. Centrifugal force will keep the ball spinning inside the jar as you raise it over the book. Keep the jar spinning while you hold it all the way over the book.

How to Build Newton's Puzzler, page 52

The quarters at the 100-centimeter mark fell more slowly than the meterstick. The meterstick has its *center of gravity* at the 50-centimeter mark. All parts of the stick must fall as if they were at the center of gravity. This means that the 100-centimeter end had to fall faster to keep things even. The quarters at the 50-centimeter mark fell at the same rate as the meterstick. That's because the quarters were located at the meterstick's center of gravity.

Where Is My Penny? page 53

Have someone pour water into the cereal bowl. This will bend the light and enable you to see the penny.

How to Test This Newton Puzzler, page 55

As the candle burns, it becomes lighter and rises. According to Archimedes' principle, the candle always pushes aside its own weight of water. Your candle will try to stay at the same height above the water.

How to Build Newton's Puzzler, page 57

You can move the hoop towards you by using Bernoulli's law. Blow through the straw from above, along the rear edge of the hoop. By blowing hard, you speed up the air which lowers the air pressure on that side. Normal air pressure on the opposite side of the hoop pushes it toward you.

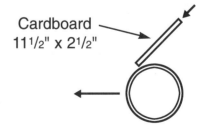

Cardboard
11½" x 2½"

Predicting Circular Segments, pages 58-60

The circle with six points does not come out as predicted. Newton doesn't know why. Many famous scientists have pondered this puzzler. So far, no one has come up with an answer. This is one unsolved puzzler waiting for your solution.

TLC10138 Copyright © Teaching & Learning Company, Carthage, IL 62321-0010